Move to Portugal... Why Not?

A Complete Guide For Wannabe Expats

By The Expat Homes Team

Why Portugal?

Note to readers, March 2023: The updates to this edition are clearly marked in all-caps with the word **UPDATED 2021 or UPDATED 2022 or UPDATED 2023.** The reason we have kept the updates and labeled them this way is to create a historical record because there is all sorts of outdated information floating around online.

It seems the world is moving on and COVID is becoming less of an international focus as more data around vaccines and lockdowns emerges, but time will tell what happens with all of that.

Some of the updates are not related to COVID and pandemic restrictions, but many of them are. We will do our best to update this book when dramatic changes happen. If you see something that needs clarification or seems wrong to you, please feel free to reach out info@espatriati.com and we will do our best to help you...no charge.

This guide is intended to give you everything you need to know about moving to Portugal **to a point.** Immigration rules for *any* country are changing all the time and Portugal is no exception. The general information, links and suggestions in this guide are presented in a way so you have a general idea of what you are looking for, and can visit the appropriate websites to get the latest information. Links are included when possible and appropriate.

So here we go!

It is difficult to find anyone who dislikes Portugal after visiting. What's not to like? Portugal is home to top-notch hiking, surfing, sailing, golf, food, weather...the list goes on.

The rich culture and overly friendly people are noticeable throughout Portugal. The relaxed lifestyle and physical safety are also big draws for many expats, and the low cost of living is the icing on the cake. (A note for the US citizens: Portugal is the fourth safest country in the world, and the United States ranks number 122...you can share that with your concerned friends and family when they hear about your relocation plans.)

Portugal is a popular relocation destination for people of all ages, although it has become particularly popular with retirees from all over the world. It is particularly popular as a retirement destination for those from non-EU countries such as the US, Canada and now the UK (although the Brits are now having a different experience moving to Portugal post-Brexit).

The citizenship by investment program (aka Golden Visa program) was launched in 2012 as a way to attract wealthy foreigners to Portugal by making it easy to obtain citizenship by investment. Of all the countries in the EU, Portugal is one of the simplest and easiest for foreigners to eventually obtain citizenship.

UPDATE 2023: The Golden Visa program in Portugal has been terminated.

Some history

Portugal is one of the oldest countries in the world, obtaining their independence from Spain in the year 1279. Portugal was a global powerhouse at one point and had colonies on all continents (except Antarctica, of course). Lisbon is one of the oldest capital cities in Europe dating about 400 years before the existence of the Roman Empire.

The church became an important institution in Portuguese life after the fall of the Roman Empire and the church maintains a large degree of influence over life in Portugal today.

Some of the most famous explorers in world history were from Portugal. Fernando Magellan was one of the first to navigate the globe, Vasco da Gama's explorations established the trade route from Europe to India and Bartolome Dias was one of the first to sail around Africa.

As a result of Portugal's naval dominance at the time, they created a handful of colonies. Some of those colonies are well-known Portuguese colonies, such as Brazil, and others are not quite as well known, such as Mozambique. Portugal and Spain were fierce rivals during the colonization years from the 1200s to the 1600s and they fought many battles over various issues.

Fun fact: Rio de Janeiro, Brazil was the capital of Portugal (yes, you read that correctly) from 1808-1821. This was due to a series of crises in Portugal including Napoleon taking control of the mainland for a period of time.

Navigating daily live in Portugal

This section is a quick and dirty overview of the things that expats frequently encounter during their planning and transition to live in Portugal. It is not comprehensive, but it is a good collection of answers to frequently asked questions.

Language

Portuguese is one of the most widely-spoken languages in the world. It is the official language of nine countries and has an estimated 230 million speakers. English is spoken in Portugal, but you should learn some Portuguese if you are planning to move there.

Important note: Some of the popular language learning apps (like DuoLingo) teach Brazilian Portuguese instead of the dialect spoken in Portugal. Be careful about which one you select before you get too deep into the language lessons. Memrise is an app that offers the dialect of Portuguese spoken in Portugal. One-on-one language lessons are also a good idea if you need some help or want to accelerate your learning, and they are offered FOR FREE in big cities such as Lisbon.

You can "get by" for a long time in Portugal without learning Portuguese, but you should learn Portuguese because it is the official language! You will be showing respect by putting effort into learning the language.

A little bit of effort to use Portuguese will go over well with the locals even if they switch to English after you start speaking (this applies to the native language of any foreign country). Of course, life is easier to manage if you speak the local language.

Plus, those who are pursuing Portuguese citizenship will need to pass a Portuguese language proficiency test when the time comes. This is a good place to learn about language test subjects if it applies to your situation.

Weather

Most of Portugal's weather is very pleasant, most of the time. The Atlantic Ocean is responsible for keeping things moderate. It's never too hot and never too cold (by most opinions).

Of course, the seasons will have an effect on the weather, but geography is a bigger determining factor. If you like it to be generally hotter, head south to the Algarve. If you like it to be generally cooler, head north to Porto. If you like it somewhere in the middle, stay... somewhere in the middle.

Those who decide to live in the northern regions of the country frequently find that the winters can be cold inside their homes. Central heating is rare in the older homes (of which there are many), so space heaters and extra layers are the preferred ways to keep warm.

Driving

It is possible to get around Portugal without owning a car. For those who wish to obtain a Portuguese driver's license, it takes a little work. Bureaucracy!

You will need to complete the process to exchange your license for a Portuguese license in the first six months after your residency becomes official. Failure to do so could earn you some fines if you are caught driving, and you will have to complete the licensing process from scratch if you miss the window in which you can exchange your original license for a Portuguese.

To exchange your license, you will need your original license, proof from the Portuguese consulate that your license is legitimate, an official driving record (with apostille) from your home country, NIF number, your residency permit, the original document showing confirmation of your address and a health certificate that states you are healthy enough to drive. All of this documentation needs to be original—copies will not be accepted.

National holidays (translation: expect things to be closed and/or expect parades / related celebrations)

January 1	New Year's Day
Changes	Carnival
Changes	Good Friday
Changes	Easter
April 25	Liberty Day
May 1	Labor Day
June 10	Portugal Day
Changes	Corpus Christi
August 15	Assumption Day
October 5	Proclamation of Portuguese Republic
November 1	All Saints' Day
December 1	Restoration of Portuguese Independence
December 8	Feast of Immaculate Conception
December 25	Christmas Day

Wine

Wine has been around Portugal for about two thousand years. The most famous Portuguese wine, Port, was first called by that name in the 1600s. The grapes are grown in Northern

Portugal in the Douro Valley. A popular legend is that the northern city of Porto was named after the wine instead of the other way around.

For the uninitiated, Port is usually a deep red color and has a sweet taste to it. It is popular all over the world and you will encounter it at stores and restaurants everywhere you go in Portugal. The traditional methods used for making Port wine are still largely used today, with a few minor technological advances. One unique feature of Port is that it is fortified with brandy. This gives it a higher alcohol content and a corresponding boozy taste.

Food

One of the best parts about moving to a new place is learning how the locals live. A big part of that is food! Everybody needs to eat, and many cultural experiences will have a food component of some sort.

Due to Portugal's geography, it is no surprise that seafood is a main staple throughout the country. The weather and landscape make Portuguese cuisine varied and delightful. There is plenty of land available to grow crops and raise animals. Easy access to the Atlantic Ocean completes the seafood part of the equation.

Salted cod known as bacalhau is the national dish of Portugal. You will see it everywhere. How the Portuguese began eating bacalhau is a source of historical debate. Cod is a cheap fish and not native to Portuguese waters—it comes from the North Atlantic. So why do the Portuguese love it so much?

One theory is the Vikings would bring it with them to trade and it became popular that way. Another theory is that Portuguese explorers preserved cod with salt during their long voyages and sold the excess fish to the locals when they returned home. However it happened, bacalhau is here to stay. There are reportedly 365 ways to cook bacalhau, one for each day of the year.

Pets

If you are coming from another EU country and bringing a pet (dog, cat or ferret) with you, proof of rabies vaccination is all you will need. Your veterinarian in your home country can attest to the rabies vaccination in your pet passport.

If you are coming from outside the EU, you will also need to provide proof of rabies vaccination. Depending on your home country, there may be extra steps. Your veterinarian will be able to help you navigate the requirements.

All pets entering Portugal need to be microchipped. Pets from outside the EU will need a health certificate that is completed by a veterinarian no more than ten days before arriving in Portugal. There is no quarantine required for pets upon arrival.

Shipping items to Portugal

This is not recommended. Seriously, sell or donate everything that doesn't fit in a few suitcases and repurchase whatever you need when you arrive in Portugal. Many people will not take this advice, but you will wish you had! Remember: *It's just stuff.* Portugal has people living there who have the same needs as you and there are stores where you can buy stuff. One of the best travel hacks in the world is to remember that, "People live where you are going and they buy the same things as you."

For those who are ignoring the advice to purge their possessions, shipping them will be difficult and expensive. There is one exception to this, though. You are allowed a one-time shipment of household goods that will not be subject to import duties, BUT the shipment must arrive within 90 days of the approval of your temporary residence permit.

Heads-up! The official policy of the government is that the one-time shipment of personal household goods must arrive within 365 days. The experiences of many expats over many years have proven that the 365 day allowance is simply not true. Get your stuff there in the first 90 days or it WILL be subject to import taxes. You will not be an exception and you will not win an argument with a customs official because "you read on the website that..."

Amazon

Amazon has become so ubiquitous that it deserves a special mention. The COVID-19 crisis only accelerated their growth and they show no signs of slowing down.

There is no *direct* Amazon service in Portugal. There are several services that allow you to order from Amazon in the UK, Germany or Spain and forward yourself packages that way. It's a bit more expensive and takes more time, but it works well enough to be a viable option.

Be sure to check the insurance policy in case your package gets lost or damaged, and think twice before ordering something worth enough to get you stuck with a big import tax bill.

Banking

UPDATE 2023: Most banks in Portugal will not open accounts for foreigners UNTIL they have a residence card. This creates a chicken and egg problem. You are still required to have a Portuguese bank account for your visa application, but you can't get the visa until you have the bank account.

The best solution here is to try a few different branches of large banks (the less-busy ones seem to be the most cooperative) OR hire a lawyer to do it for you with a power of attorney. Giving *anyone* a power of attorney over a bank account is a bad idea in my opinion, but it might be the only option for some.

You used to be able to open a bank account in Portugal with nothing more than a valid passport, residential address and some cash for an initial deposit. It is now a bit more difficult. You will need an NIF number and you will need to be physically present in Portugal in order to open the account. (The exception here is if you give someone in Portugal a power of attorney to open the account for you. You should understand the risks of signing a power of attorney before considering this option…it can end badly if you aren't careful.)

How do you get an NIF number? You can do it in-person (plan for delays on getting that appointment due to the COVID backlog of appointments), or you can do it online with one of these two services: NIFOnline.pt or Bordr.io. The process can take up to a month based on recent reports (March 2022).

A bank account with a Portuguese bank is now *required* to submit with your residency application. Many online banks that allow you to remotely open accounts are not accepted because they are not Portuguese banks (N26, Revolut, etc.).

UPDATED 2021: Furthermore, your bank account must be fully funded with at least enough money to qualify for your level of visa for one year (more on the minimum amounts later). The old rule was you could show your balance in a bank account from your home country, but they now require the money to be in Portugal in an approved Portuguese bank.

Some Portuguese banks were previously allowing remote account opening, but that seems to be going the way of the dodo bird. No more! You may find exceptions, but most reports as of today suggest that it's a waste of time to try this approach. You'll need to be on the ground in Portugal with your NIF number in hand, and you can open a bank account during an exploratory trip--no need for a permanent address in Portugal.

Having a Portuguese bank and significant money deposited in your account may also help with your visa application process, (instead of showing big funds in a foreign account). It's a little thing, but it might help if there are other factors on your application that are working against you.

Many stores, restaurants, etc. do not accept credit cards. You will want to have access to a debit card that is accepted worldwide to make purchases and access cash at the ATM. It is a good idea to have a few different payment options with you if you are planning to maintain a credit card in your home country (many expats do this simply for the points).

Some popular banks in Portugal are Activobank, Millennium and Banco Best. As always, it is wise to shop around and pay attention to the fine print so you don't incur any bank fees. Revolut is not based in Portugal, but it is popular with expats and makes international money transfers very easy.

Crime and safety

Portugal is one of the safest countries in the world! Crime rates are low, and violent crime rates are especially low. The crime that does exist is (surprise, surprise) mostly petty crime and mostly occurs in the tourist areas. This is the standard situation in many parts of Europe that are popular with tourists.

As always, a little common sense goes a long way. Don't flash your money around in public, don't leave your valuables unattended, etc.

One of the most interesting social experiments in modern history took effect in Portugal in 2001. In the 1990s, heroin and HIV were major problems in Portugal. Addicts were everywhere and HIV infections were the worst in all of Europe.

Fast-forward to 2001 when Portugal decriminalized all drug usage in the country. That doesn't mean you have retail stores selling drugs in the open like Amsterdam or one-third of the US, but there aren't criminal penalties for drug possession or usage.

The money that was previously spent on drug law enforcement and policing drug-related crimes was redirected to social programs to help those who have drug problems.

The result? Portugal is now the safest country in Europe and one of the safest in the world. Drug usage, HIV transmission and homelessness all steadily plummeted after the decriminalization in 2001.

Regardless of your personal feelings about drug usage, the results are clear: Decriminalizing drug usage caused a dramatic reduction in crime and a dramatic improvement in public health in Portugal.

That's not what the fear-mongering Western media outlets would have you believe, is it? Shame on them.

The recreational drug users in Portugal can do as they please and those who have addiction issues can easily access social services to help them kick their habits. The experiment is hailed as one of the greatest public health success stories in modern world history.

Popular cities and areas

Portugal is a small country when you consider the total land mass. It is about the size of the US state of Maine, or about a third of the size of Italy. The country consists of the mainland and two island chains.

Despite the relatively small size of Portugal, there are dramatic differences in the different areas of the country. With beaches, mountains, countryside and dense urban areas, there is something for everyone.

This section provides an overview of some of the most popular places in Portugal. It is far from comprehensive as there are dozens of small cities and areas that are perfectly suitable as well. I wanted to provide a quick overview without turning this section into a separate book by itself.

A common question from those considering moving to Portugal is, "Where should I live?" That is a legitimate question, but it is hard to get an answer from someone else because there are so many variables. The best way to learn where would be good for you is to make an exploratory trip to Portugal and spend time in a handful of cities to try them out.

Lisbon (Lisboa)

Lisbon is the largest city in Portugal with a population of roughly three million, and it is also the capital. It has a "big, little city" feel to it. The entire city is easily navigable through taxis, public transportation or walking.

In Lisbon, you will find all the restaurant, cafe and bar options you could possibly want. The establishments are open well into the evening hours and late nights are common for social activity.

There are a few great beach options in or near Lisbon as well. They are all easily accessible via public transportation or a quick drive. Because of the geography, you can find calm waters or raging surf within an hour of Lisbon. There are four distinct coastlines, each offering something different.

Biggest complaint about Lisbon: It is expensive compared to most of the rest of Portugal.

Porto

The second largest city with a population of 240,000 in the city proper and 2.4 million in the metropolitan area. It is located in the northern part of the country which is a bit cooler than the rest of Portugal. Many people compare the climate in Porto to the climate in Northern California.

Porto has a large and active expat community and the cost of living is lower than Lisbon or the Algarve. It is a popular destination due to the food scene, architecture and relaxed atmosphere. Porto also enjoys easy access to a variety of outdoor activities.

Biggest complaint about Porto: Weather.

Faro

On the other end of the climate spectrum and the other end of the country from Porto is Faro. Faro is the largest city in the Algarve with a population of roughly 68,000. The total population in the Algarve region (in which Faro is the largest city) is about 125,000.

Beach life is a major draw for Faro and the rest of the Algarve. Many expats enjoy the warm weather all year and the relaxed attitude that comes with life in the Algarve. Faro is big enough to have good options for dining and activities, but not big enough to be overwhelming.

Biggest complaint about The Algarve: Tourists.

Cascais

Cascais is a popular spot for expats. It was originally a fishing village and is large enough to have all the big city amenities, but not big enough to be overwhelming. It is located on the Portuguese Riviera and is an easy journey from Lisbon by train, bus or car (about 32 kilometers / 20 miles).

The outdoor activities are plentiful in Cascais. There are great hiking, golfing, beach and water activity options in and around Cascais. The city has not lost its history as a fishing village. Fishing is still a large part of the local economy.

Biggest complaint about Cascais: Prices for some things are seemingly outrageous compared to the rest of Portugal (lots of wealthy expats live in Cascais and the locals have figured out they can charge big prices).

Costa da Caparica

This one is a sleeper. Most tourists don't visit here, although it is popular with the locals. The coastline itself stretches about 24 kilometers and the resort town of the same name is situated in the northern portion of the coastline.

Most of the development and tourist options are located in or near the town. The southern portion of the coastline is less developed and a large section of it is part of a protected nature preserve.

For those of you who like to sunbathe in the buff, Costa da Caparica is also home to Portugal's original nudist beach. Reminder: It's never polite to stare.

Surfing is popular at Costa da Caparica. There are companies that offer lessons and rent surfing equipment. The waves are good for beginner and intermediate surfers.

The Estoril Coast

The Estoril coastline is probably the most popular coastline in Portugal. It contains eighteen unique beaches and is located just west of Lisbon. The easy access for the biggest population hub and the variety of beaches make it a popular destination for tourists and locals alike.

All of the beaches are easy to reach using public transportation. The Estoril coast is also the home of the "Portuguese Riviera." King Luis I made the coast popular in the 1800s when he made it his summer home. Of course, the people followed his lead because everybody wants to be close to the king.

There are a few resort towns along the Estoril Coast. Moving west from Lisbon, you will travel through Paço de Arcos, Oeiras, Carcavelos, Parede and Cascais. Cascais is where the train stops and it is a larger city with a historic city center. There are plenty of lodging and restaurant options in Cascais.

Serra de Sintra Coast

The Serra de Sintra coast is located along the Atlantic Ocean north of Cascais. The entire coast is exposed to the ocean and is a popular destination for hardcore water sports (namely surfing) and hiking. The wind can be intense and the soaring cliffs are a sight to behold.

Praia das Maçãs and Azenhas do Mar are two resort towns along the coast that offer the usual cafes and restaurants, along with many notable vantage points that are good for photographers and those who just want to take it all in.

Cabo da Roca is the westernmost point in mainland Europe and is located in Serra de Sintra. Don't be one of those people who falls into the ocean because they are trying to get the perfect selfie to post on Instagram. Just look at it from a safe distance.

Aveiro

Aviero is located in the northern part of Portugal between Porto and Coimbra. It is a popular destination for tourists who enjoy the canals running throughout the city and the classic architecture. There are plenty of historic and cultural locations to visit in Aveiro as well.

Aviero is located on a lagoon and is home to the tallest lighthouse in Portugal. There are several beaches to choose from that are also popular with surfers for those who wish to venture out of the city a bit.

Coimbra

Coimbra sits on the Mondego River, which was a catalyst for much of Coimbra's history. It was the capital of Portugal for about 100 years and the river made it an important location between Lisbon and Braga.

Coimbra is perhaps best known for the University of Coimbra, which is famous for its long list of successful alumni and beautiful architecture. The university drives much of the economy in Coimbra and helps keep a vibrant nightlife scene alive.

There are several medieval churches that are popular destinations for residents and tourists alike. The largest national park in Portugal is called Serra da Estrela and is an easy drive from Coimbra.

Azores

Officially known as the Autonomous Region of the Azores, the island archipelago lies 1500 kilometers / 930 miles west of Lisbon. The region consists of nine volcanic islands and has evidence of human inhabitation dating back 2000 years.

The largest city in the Azores is Ponta Delgada. Tourism drives most of the economy in the Azores and many residents are employed in the service industry. There are also healthy agriculture, livestock and fishing industries in the Azores.

Fun fact: The Azores are some of the tallest mountains on the planet. The measurements are taken from the base of the mountains on the floor of the ocean.

Madeira Islands

The Madeira Islands are located about 480 kilometers / 300 miles from Morocco. There are two inhabited islands (Madeira and Porto Santo) and two uninhabited island groups (Desertas and the Selvagens).

Madeira has a long history as a shipping stop for those traveling by boat. Madeira Island is the largest island and home to the capital city of Funchal.

The mild weather and warm temperature make it a pleasant place to be at all times of the year. Along with the fairly close island of Tenerife in the Canary Islands, the weather is described as "eternal spring." Agriculture and wine are the main drivers of the economy and the largest exports.

Visas, residency and citizenship

Visiting Portugal requires a visa or passport. Citizens of countries in the European Community (Schengen and a few others) can enter without a visa. All visitors to Portugal will need at least six months of validity remaining on their passports to be admitted into the country. Some countries have visa free access to Portugal, so check with your embassy to see if you qualify.

The government advises a forwarding or return ticket, or proof of the financial means to support you during your stay. Even though that is their official stance, most border control agents do not ask visitors for proof of either. Better safe than sorry, though. Getting turned away at the border because of some small oversight on your part is never fun.

Portugal joined the Schengen zone in 1995.

Schengen Area

The Schengen Area in Europe consists of 26 countries. They all agreed to abolish border control and passport checks with the other member countries. Anyone who has a visa to one of the member countries can travel freely to any of the other member countries. Here's the full list:

Austria
Belgium
Czech Republic
Denmark
Estonia
Finland
France

Germany
Greece
Hungary
Iceland
Italy
Latvia
Liechtenstein
Lithuania
Luxembourg
Malta
Netherlands
Norway
Poland
Portugal
Slovakia
Slovenia
Spain
Sweden
Switzerland

As of early 2020, there are also five countries petitioning to join Schengen—Ireland, Bulgaria, Croatia, Cyprus and Romania.

All Schengen members are part of the EU, but not all EU countries are part of Schengen. As you can see, Portugal and its neighbors are all Schengen members.

Travel to the Schengen zone is limited to 90 days out of every 180 days for anyone who does not have a proper residency visa for one of the Schengen countries. The 90 day limit is a rolling number, so you can't leave for a day to a non-Schengen country and return to Schengen to restart the clock. Once you have spent 90 days in Schengen, you will need to leave for at least 90 days before you can legally return.

Also, be very careful about trying to game the system here. They pay attention at the borders when you enter and exit. If you are consistently doing something like spending 87 days in Portugal, leaving for exactly three months, then spending another 85 days, etc., it will look suspicious and you may get flagged. And by "flagged," I mean labeled an illegal immigrant and banned from the country (and the rest of Schengen).

Some people have stayed 85+ days every three months for years with no problems, and others get grilled by border control for doing the same thing. Our opinion is it's not worth trying to get away with any funny business here. Either go through the process and become an official resident, or understand that you may eventually be in some hot water if someone believes you are "living" in Portugal illegally.

The path from residency to citizenship

Once you have a proper residency permit that shows you live in a Schengen country, your travel throughout Schengen will not be restricted, BUT there is one caveat.

You are required to be in Portugal for at least eight months per year for the first two years of your residence permit. They way they phrase it is 16 of 24 months in Portugal with no absence longer than six months. (Read: They don't want you getting a residence permit in Portugal, then spending all your time in some other Schengen country).

Portugal has a path to citizenship through legal residency. After five years of legal residency with one of the temporary visas, you can begin the process to obtain long-term residency. After six years, you can apply for citizenship.

It takes three years for those pursuing citizenship through marriage to a Portuguese citizen.

And once you have Portuguese citizenship, there will be no requirement for the amount of time you need to spend in Portugal. You will be free to roam.

EU citizens

Moving to Portugal as an EU citizen is simple. You don't need a special visa to do it, although you will need to apply for permanent residency if you are staying longer than three months.

EU citizens will have to provide proof of their status as a student, employee, self-employed person or pensioner. The main governmental concerns with the residency documentation are evidence of adequate health insurance coverage, and proof of the financial means to support yourself.

For non-EU citizens, the path to proper residency in Portugal is a bit more complex.

Golden Visa

UPDATED 2023: In late February, the Golden Visa program was officially terminated in Portugal. This was due to pressure from the EU to keep people from "undesirable" countries from getting EU access, and due to political pressure inside Portugal to get the cost of housing under control for the locals.

The easiest way for non-EU citizens to obtain residency in Portugal is also the path that requires the most money. Portugal has become well-known for their visa by investment (also known as the Golden Visa).

The Golden Visa is a fast-track path to residency for those who can afford it. It comes with a one-year residency permit, which can be renewed for two-year terms. The Golden Visa holders can apply for permanent residency after five years and citizenship after six years.

At the time of this writing (**UPDATED 2022**), it costs about €5400 for the initial Golden Visa, and about €2700 for each subsequent renewal. The initial filing fee is about €540 with an additional €85 per family member. Visa fees frequently change, so be sure to double-check these numbers before you get too far into the process if you think you'll be cutting it close with the cash requirements.

Some family members can be added to the Golden Visa. Spouses, dependent children (minors or adults who are studying in Portugal), dependent parents and dependent siblings. It costs just over €5100 per person to add qualifying family members.

There are three common investment options for those who wish to obtain a Golden Visa in Portugal. You can buy a property for at least €500,000, transfer at least €1,000,000 into a Portuguese bank or create ten salaried jobs with your Portuguese company.

UPDATED 2022: There are now some geographic restrictions to the qualifying Golden Visa property investments. The general idea is Portugal wants people to invest in the less popular areas to help revive them (so, not the big city centers). We have maps from different areas that we can share with you for free if you email us info@espatriati.com.

For a quick rundown of the Golden Visa options:

- €500,000 in residential real estate in the areas where it still qualifies
- €500,000 in commercial real estate in a high-density area (including coastal areas)
- €350,000 in residential or commercial real estate that is at least 30 years old or in an urban rehabilitation area within the qualifying areas of the country
- €280,000 in residential or commercial real estate in low-density areas when the property is more than 30 years old (€350,000 minus 20%)

The "minus 20%" bit deserves some more explanation.

A property in a low density area that needed to be rehabilitated would reduce the minimum investment amount by 20%. So a €350,000 property minus €70,000 would mean you can make it happen for €280,000. The same would apply to a residential property that needed to be rehabilitated in an interior area of the country that is also low density.

To make it more fun, you can also add the cost of renovations into the total calculation. So if you purchased a qualifying property for €200,000 and spent €80,000 on renovations, that would work too.

There are also a few less-common investment options that qualify for the Golden Visa—at least €250,000 invested in Portuguese culture, arts or heritage, €350,000 in scientific research in Portugal, €350,000 for a property that's at least 30 years old in an urban "regeneration" area or €500,000 invested in a small business in Portugal.

In any of the investment scenarios, you will need to hang onto the investment for at least five years. There is a potential tax advantage, too. For Golden Visa holders who spend fewer than 183 days per year in Portugal, they will not be taxed in Portugal on their worldwide income.

Residence visa

The residence visa is issued to those who intend to officially move to Portugal for the long-term. This visa is good for four months and is issued before arrival. It allows the visa holders to make up to multiple trips outside of Portugal during the four month period (if needed) to complete the process for a proper residence permit.

D1 visa

The D1 visa is for those who will be working for an employer in Portugal. The employer has to apply to the government in order to be allowed to offer a job that qualifies for this type of visa.

The challenges with this type of visa are that the employer has to demonstrate that they could not fill the role with a Portuguese person or other EU citizen, and they have to document that they advertised the opening and interviewed Portuguese and/or EU citizens (who were not qualified).

D2 visa

The D2 visa is designed for entrepreneurs who wish to move to Portugal to start a business. The term used for starting a business in this case is "an investing activity." You don't have to plan for a massive, multinational corporation--a small to medium business is suitable. The D2 visa can also be used if you have an existing company you would like to relocate to Portugal.

In order to qualify for the D2 visa, you will need to provide a business plan, proof of the viability of your business, an explanation of why you are choosing Portugal and proof that you have the financial means to sustain yourself in Portugal.

Most people who might qualify for the D2 visa prefer to go for the D7 visa instead. Why? You will need to prove your ability to financially support yourself with the D2 visa anyway. There are special cases where the D2 visa would make sense, but many times the D7 is the easier way to go.

D3 visa

The D3 visa is for foreigners who have unique skills that are valuable in the marketplace. This is also known as the "highly-skilled" visa.

In order to qualify for this visa, you must have a letter of employment from a Portuguese company that shows a salary higher than 1.5 times the minimum wage. You will also need to demonstrate that you have specific skills that are rare, or that you hold an advanced degree in your regulated field of work.

D4 visa

The D4 visa is a student visa for stays in Portugal that are longer than 90 days. It can be used for studying, paid internships and unpaid internships. Those who are studying with the D4 must maintain passing grades in the classes and at least 75% attendance.

D5 visa

The D5 visa is for college students who wish to advance their education. It is similar to the D4 (the only real difference is the level in which a person is studying) and it also requires a minimum 75% attendance rate.

D6 visa

The D6 is the family reunification visa. It can be a bit tricky to use the D6. As of mid-2023, the appointments to request D6 visas are about 12 months into the future, and it is difficult to get one in the first place.

Anyone with legal residency or citizenship in Portugal can apply with the D6 to bring spouses, dependent children (up to age 18) or dependent parents (over age 65).

D7 visa

The D7 visa is designed for people who can support themselves in Portugal with their savings, investment income and/or pension income. Basically, the Portuguese government just wants you to prove that you won't end-up destitute in Portugal.

The amount of money you will need depends on the length of your visa. You will need to be able to prove the minimum amounts in passive income OR savings and investments per year for the visa you are requesting **(UPDATED 2023)**

- €9120 for the first adult
- €4560 for the second adult

It is best if you can show income, savings or investments that exceed the minimum required amounts. It is risky for your application to be cutting it close, and it is risky for your happiness in Portugal to be cutting it close! Portugal is generally inexpensive for most people moving from the US, UK or Canada, but it's no fun to live without a financial cushion of some sort.

Some people have been able to secure a D7 visa by showing proof of regular income from an "online" or "remote" job. The D7 is not designed to be issued for those people, but some consulates and embassies may allow it if you can provide the proper documentation. The word on the street is it takes a bit of luck to get a D7 this way and there's no rhyme or reason to who is approved or denied through this method. If this path is your only option and you are in a hurry to move to Portugal, go ahead and give it a shot.

D8 visa

UPDATED 2023: The D8 visa is also known as the "digital nomad" visa. It is specifically tailored for those who have regular income from a remote job outside of Portugal..

The D8 functions much like the D7 (where many remote workers were having success in the past by massaging their applications to fit the requirements).

The D8 visa can be for as little as one year, and requires regular income from a job outside of Portugal. You will need to provide documentation of the work contract and a history of salary payments (usually three months' worth of bank statements will be sufficient).

One interesting development has been reports of people applying for the D7 and being granted a D8 at the discretion of the immigration employees. There seems to be no rhyme or reason for this and no real way to control which one you get.

The basic requirements for the D8 are similar to those of the D7--financial proof that you can sustain yourself, a clean criminal record from your home country, applying from an embassy in your country of residence and evidence of a

12-month lease or proof of ownership of a habitable property in Portugal.

Temporary stay visa

A temporary stay visa is good for one year. There are specific ways to be granted a temporary stay visa:

- Work for a Portuguese employer lasting longer than 90 days but not longer than one year
- Medical treatment
- Medical treatment for a family member
- Official training and/or work with the World Trade Organization or a World Trade Organization-related entity
- Verified work as an independent contractor
- Approved scientific or academic work
- Approved amateur sports activity
- Seasonal work
- Academic studies from an approved institution

Work visa

Employment at a level that will allow you to meet the minimum financial requirements for subsistence is an option as well. You will need a proof of employment from an employer along with some financial documentation from them showing their ability to pay you.

Keep in mind that salaries in Portugal are generally low (average wage €580 per month) and jobs for foreigners can be difficult to obtain. If you are pursuing a work visa, the way to do it is by securing the job and getting the go-ahead from your employer to apply before you arrive in Portugal.

Seasonal work visa

Maybe you want to visit Portugal and support yourself with some seasonal work while you are there. There is a special seasonal work visa that allows for a stay longer than 90 days when you qualify.

There is a large eco-minded population in Portugal and many people are working on projects involving farming and sustainability. Finding work on a farm shouldn't be too hard on any exploratory trips you make to Portugal.

There are several categories of seasonal work that qualify for the seasonal work visa.

- Agriculture, livestock, hunting, fishing and forestry
- Hospitality (restaurants and hotels)
- Food industry and tobacco
- Retail
- Construction
- Land transportation

Marriage, partner or family reunification visa

Portuguese citizenship by marriage is available after three years or legal marriage or "legally recognized" cohabitation. Be prepared to show proof of cohabitation if you are going this route. Also, divorce after obtaining citizenship via marriage does not affect your citizenship.

Family reunification is designed for couples where one is a Portuguese citizen and the other is not. The documentation needed includes proof of your partner's citizenship along with all the other standard requirements.

Visa documentation

This is the required documentation for any visas other than tourist or transit visas. There are some slight variations depending on your particular visa (such as a letter of employment if you are applying for a work visa), but they all require the following:

- Two recent passport photos
- A valid passport or other travel document with at least six months left before expiration
- Proof of the means to financially support yourself for the duration of your visa
- Proof of adequate accommodation (lease or purchase agreement for a property)
- Permission for a criminal record check
- Criminal record check from your home country (like FBI for US citizens)
- Proof of health insurance
- Proof of registration with the local tax authority
- Completed forms and fees
- Marriage certificate (if applicable)

- A personal statement explaining why you want to live in Portugal and any other pertinent details about your situation (if applicable)

E-visa portal

In an effort to make the visa application process easier for everyone, the government launched an online visa system in early 2020. The new portal provides the following services for visa applicants and holders:

- Registration
- Password change
- Modification of personal data
- Access to the history of all your visa requests
- The online visa application is preceded by a questionnaire that will help you determine the type of visa you need
- Possibility to attach documents to your visa application

A note about dual citizenship

Portugal allows for dual citizenship, but your home country may not allow it. Some countries require you to renounce your citizenship if you obtain citizenship in another country. Check with your home country's government to learn the rules for your situation.

Jobs

Unemployment is fairly high in Portugal, although there is still strong demand for highly-skilled workers in fields such as technology and medicine.

Wages are low in Portugal compared to countries such as the US, UK and Canada. The minimum wage is lower than many of the other European Union countries.

The minimum wage calculation is a bit goofy. The minimum wage is set at a certain rate (€705 a month as of 2022). That amount is multiplied by 14 to account for an annual Christmas bonus and holiday bonus, then the total is divided by 12 to figure the monthly payment amount.

Although the minimum wage is the lowest in Western Europe, the median salary in Portugal is about €2600 per month. The minimum wage is enough to live because the cost of living is much lower in Portugal than most of Western Europe as well.

Every full-time worker in Portugal is given at least twenty-two days of paid holiday time per year, in addition to the nine public holidays.

Work permits are required for those who wish to work in Portugal and are not from a European Union or European Economic Area country. Those from the EU and EEA must apply for a residence permit within six months of arriving in Portugal even though they do not need a work permit in order to start working.

Obtaining a work permit as a non-EU or non-EEA citizen can be challenging. There are a few steps that must be taken in order to comply with the residency and employment laws which will likely involve multiple trips to Portugal. There is the added complexity of finding a suitable job when Portuguese companies are more inclined to hire Portuguese citizens.

One preferred path for obtaining a work permit is to secure a job with a multinational company that has offices in Portugal and transfer with a job already in place.

Highly skilled workers in any field who can demonstrate that they have specialized knowledge will have an easier time securing a work permit from a Portuguese company.

Many expats choose to pursue remote work while living in Portugal, either as freelancers or as part of a company that is based elsewhere. Those who choose this route will still need to complete all the necessary paperwork and registrations in order to legally be allowed to stay beyond the limits of a tourist visa.

Transportation

There are ten airports located throughout Portugal. The three international airports are located in Lisbon, Porto and Faro. Over two dozen airlines service Portugal and TAP Portugal is the country's main airline with both domestic and international flights.

UPDATED 2021, STILL GOING IN 2022: While it is our cynical belief that all commercial airlines are different degrees of bad and getting worse every year, TAP has received some especially negative feedback lately that affects expats and wannabe expats. They have been canceling flights at the last-minute without apology, which has consequences for those who are relying on TAP to get to Portugal. It is annoying but necessary to plan for hassles, delays and cancellations from TAP for now.

There is a robust public transportation system in the major urban areas in Portugal. There are many photos of the funicular in Lisbon that carry passengers up the steep hills. The bus, tram and rail lines connect all the cities in the country.

People moving from car-centric areas of the world (many US citizens) can't imagine life without a car until they get to Portugal. "But I *need* a car!" is a common statement from many, but the public transportation system has converted many car people into public transportation people. Give it a try. Carless life is good. Rent one when you really do need it.

The underground train system (metro) is wonderful for most travel in Lisbon and Porto. Those two cities are the only ones with a metro system. Tickets and passes are available at the ticket counters and machines located in the metro stations.

The rail network in Portugal is robust. There is a high-speed train that runs between Braga to Faro, stopping at Porto, Coimbra and Lisbon. There are also many regional, intercity and commuter trains. It is wise to purchase train tickets in advance either at a station or online, especially for the inter-city and regional train routes. There are also a few international train lines connecting to locations in Spain and France.

The bus, tram and funicular lines make transportation around the larger cities easy and inexpensive. There are also coach services that run between some of the major cities and popular areas.

Taxis and services such as Uber, Taxify and Cabify are popular options for getting around as well. There are plenty of options in the urban centers, and limited options in the rural areas.

The major highways are well-maintained throughout Portugal. Traveling by private automobile is a popular option for many, but it is not necessary for most people. There are also some boat and ferry routes that connect various parts of the country.

Housing & Property

Fun fact: Of all the Western European countries, Portugal has the highest percentage of people living in rural areas.

For some people, buying a property in Portugal is their path to residency and eventual citizenship. The Golden Visa (or visa by investment) is a popular option, especially with the well-to-do from countries such as the US, Canada and the UK.

It is common for foreigners to buy property in Portugal as a seasonal retreat or an investment. The strategy to use a property for part of the year and rent it out the rest of the time is a popular option, especially with those who plan to retire in Portugal someday but aren't ready to pull the trigger just yet.

Whether you are buying as investment or simply to solve your shelter needs, there are some things you should know about property in Portugal. About 75% of Portuguese citizens own their homes.

There are no restrictions on foreign ownership of property in Portugal. Most expats prefer to rent for a while to see how much they like an area before buying a property there. The vast differences in the various parts of Portugal make the "try before you buy" approach appealing. As little as a few weeks in each place will give you a good idea of what you can expect if you were to decide to live there.

Real estate agents are involved in almost all property transactions in Portugal. There are large, international real estate brands present in Portugal, along with many smaller, independent real estate agencies. Most agents specialize in a specific geographic area and you will be able to find English-speaking agents in the urban centers and popular coastal towns.

UPDATED 2021: There is no such thing as an MLS (multiple listing service) in Portugal, and anyone can print business cards saying they are real estate agents to become a real estate agent. It is commonly referred to as "the wild west" by foreigners. The best way to find a reliable agent is to get referrals from other expats. We can help with recommendations at no cost at espatriati.com. Send us an email and we'll set you up with a few good agent options for the area(s) you are considering. Email portugal@espatriati.com with the areas you are considering.

The suburbs surrounding the large urban areas (Lisbon and Porto) are home to many more residents than the urban centers. Apartments are prevalent in the urban centers and single family homes are prevalent just about everywhere else.

Parts of Portugal can be damp and cold in the winter. Many homes do not have central heating (or any built-in heating) or insulation. Some homes have fireplaces, but many people rely on space heaters and layers of clothing to stay warm.

The homes are classified with codes that look gibberish if you don't know what they mean (you'll see the code in ads and property websites).

They use codes of T0, T1, T2, T3 and so on to describe the number of bedrooms in an apartment. A T0 apartment is a studio. A T3 apartment is a three bedroom apartment. If there are small rooms that could be used as bedrooms, they are classified with a +. A two bedroom apartment with an additional small room is T2+1. Single family houses use a similar system, but they use a V instead of a T. A two bedroom house with two small additional rooms is V2+2.

Renters

Tenants have significant rights in Portugal. As a renter, that may make you feel good. As a landlord, that may make you a little nervous.

All rentals in Portugal are required to have written leases (even short-term leases). The leases outline the standard terms you would expect:

- Who pays for utilities
- When the rent is due
- What common spaces are available for tenants to use
- What happens to the deposit at the end of the lease term
- If pets are allowed
- The number of people who can live there
- What are the conditions for ending the lease early
- Who takes care of things like the lawn or bushes or pool maintenance

It is important that you understand what you are signing even if that means hiring a translator to translate the lease document for you.

One thing you might not have considered to check: Does the house have heating? It won't matter much in the warm parts of the country or during the summer months, but many homes in Portugal do NOT have heating. They are designed to stay cool in the summer, which means they also stay cool in the winter. The cold houses are a common complaint from expats who are spending their first winter in Portugal and are caught off guard.

The best places to find rentals are on estate agent websites in the areas where you are considering living, and paid advertising websites such as Facebook (yuck...scammers) or the local newspaper websites. There is no national website that lists properties for rent like you find in the US, UK or Canada. You may also have some luck by walking or driving the neighborhoods in the areas you like to look for "arrendar" (for rent) signs in windows. We don't do rentals at espatriati.com, but we might know some rental agents who can help. Email portugal@espatriati.com if you would like some expat friendly suggestions.

Construction and renovation

Renovating old properties in Portugal can be an appealing option for those who have some experience. It is not recommended for those who have never undertaken a renovation project.

One of the golden visa options is to purchase a property worth at least €350,000 that needs to be rehabilitated. There are rules around which properties are allowed for visa purposes, so be sure to check on the nitty gritty details if you plan to go that route.

Building a property from scratch is another option. Before embarking upon a brand-new construction project, you will want to double check the local zoning laws for your property and the type and size of construction that's allowed. Some property is zoned agricultural where you would not be allowed to build a house.

There are also size considerations in many places that govern how big of a house you can build on a lot, and other things like whether you are allowed to put in a pool. The local town council will be able to guide you on what's allowed and not allowed for any piece of property you are considering.

Permits for any major works will be required from the local council. The permits have a time limit to them (usually one year), so don't dilly dally if you are granted a permit. Minor renovations that don't change the footprint of the house or are internal renovations usually do not require special permitting.

Once the renovation or construction project is complete, you will need to alert the local council to have the property revalued. The new valuation will be used to calculate your tax bills moving forward.

There are plenty of new development options in most coastal areas in Portugal. This is handy if you are looking for a new property, but don't want to deal with the headaches and hassles of building it yourself. Be sure to check the reputation of the developer before committing to anything.

Mortgages

Mortgages for expats are difficult to obtain, but not impossible. The preferred funding methods are cash, or a credit line attached to your assets in your home country. Some banks will consider your credit score from your home country and others do not. In either case, they will do a comprehensive review of your financial situation before they approve you for a mortgage.

The maximum age allowed for you to have a mortgage attached to your property is 75 years. So if you retire at 65 and move to Portugal, the longest term available to you would be ten years.

The down payment requirements for expat mortgages are also hefty. They can range from 30% to 50% depending on your financial situation . There may also be a life insurance requirement depending on the bank issuing the mortgage (insurance can be purchased through the banks).

UPDATED 2022: Some banks now are offering 20% down payment mortgages to foreigners even before they arrive in Portugal as official residents. We were quoted a 1.59% interest rate for a 30-year mortgage with a 20% down payment as non-residents (**UPDATED 2023:** Interest rates are now quite a bit higher than the 1.59% we were quoted a year prior. C'est la vie). Once you have residency, there may be mortgages available with a 10% down payment. However, those are rare situations, so don't count on it being true for you.

You will need to show some regular income in order to qualify for a mortgage as well. Your mortgage payment will not be able to exceed 30% of your regular monthly income.

How real estate agents work in Portugal

As a rule, every property transaction in Portugal involves real estate agents ("imobiliárias"). As a buyer, the agents don't cost you anything (the commission is paid by the seller). You might as well use them instead of banging your head against a wall trying to find a way to cut them out.

Remember: The listing agent always represents the seller, not you as the buyer. They may not be entirely honest about that part of the deal, so be careful what information you share with them and what you share with your buyer's agent while the listing agents are within earshot.

Brokerages in Portugal are required to be licensed, but there is no regulatory authority that governs agents. Most of them do not carry errors and omissions or professional indemnity insurance (there are low limits if they carry insurance at all). Warning: There are many "agents" in Portugal who operate without licenses. A reputable agent will gladly show you proof of their licensing status.

The licensing status of an agent probably won't matter much until you get to the point of writing an offer and making a deposit. At that point, you will want to be sure you are working with someone reputable (especially if they are touching or directing anything to do with your deposit).

For rentals, local estate agencies will have short-term and long-term options available for you. Many of the apartments don't make their way onto the estate agency websites, so you'll want to make friends with a few local agents who work rentals. You can also use websites such as Airbnb to find long-term housing. Pro-tip: Find housing that's available for the times you need and contact the owners before booking to see what sort of discount they will offer for a long-term tenant.

The purchase process

Once you have found a property you like and have made an offer that's accepted, there are a few moving parts that need to be carefully managed. Keep in mind the entire purchase process can take up to three months for a regular transaction when nothing goes wrong.

You should plan to hire a solicitor (lawyer) to represent you as well. This is especially important if you do not speak Portuguese and are not familiar with Portuguese laws and customs (basically, the target market for this book).

Your solicitor will help you make sure you complete all the necessary legal steps in the transaction and provide you with advice along the way. The solicitor is also responsible for creating the contracts and checking the title history and tax history to be sure there are no problems that might jeopardize the transaction.

Portuguese law requires you to hire a notary to "oversee" the transaction (notaries work for the government). The notary serves as an independent person in the middle of the transaction to make sure all the ducks are in a row regarding the title, transfer taxes, contract paperwork, local registrations, etc.

Once the contract terms are agreed upon and the title search is satisfactory, the contract becomes legally binding between the buyer and the seller. A deposit is required by the buyer at this stage. Anything from 10% to 30% is typical, and the exact amount is part of your initial contract negotiations. At this point, the property transfer taxes need to be paid to the local tax authority.

The final steps are for the buyer and seller to sign the deed in the presence of a notary who will record the deed and the balance of the purchase price to be paid to the seller. These steps happen simultaneously.

Property transfer taxes

The transfer taxes are brutal. Brace yourself.

The buyer will have to pay up to 10% of the property's purchase price as a transfer tax (depends on the price of the property). There are also registration fees, stamp duty, legal fees, and a notary fee. The total taxes and fees paid by the buyer usually total 12-14% of the purchase price.

Sellers are responsible for the real estate agent commission (4%-6%) plus VAT of 23%. There are also filing and legal fees paid by the seller.

Rental income and capital gains taxes are calculated differently for residents and non-residents. You must also register your property as a rental with the local authorities if you are using it primarily as a rental property.

Residents add rental income to their total income from other sources for the year and income pay taxes on the rate for their tax bracket. Non-residents pay income tax of 28% on any rental income. Local property taxes, repairs, maintenance and insurance can be deducted from rental income (mortgage interest cannot be deducted).

Capital gains for residents are added to their total income for the year as well and taxed at the same rate as their other income. Capital gains tax for non-residents is 28% which is paid at the time a property is sold.

There are a few exceptions to capital gains tax.

1. If the gains are reinvested in another property, only 50% of the gains are taxed.
2. If you are a tax resident in Portugal, the property is a primary residence and you purchase another primary

residence in Portugal, there will be no capital gains tax. This applies to primary residences purchased up to two years *before* or three years *after* the sale.

3. If the property was a primary residence and you reinvest the gains into another primary residence located anywhere in the EU, there will be no capital gains tax.

Healthcare

Healthcare in Portugal is public (Serviço Nacional de Saúde or SNS). The country is consistently ranked one of the best in the world for healthcare. The Portuguese have one of the longest life expectancies in the world as well. It is written in the Portuguese constitution that healthcare is a human right for any person who finds themselves needing medical care in Portugal regardless of visa or citizenship status.

The public healthcare is very good, although many expats choose to keep private insurance as well to give them more options. The private insurance policies are MUCH cheaper than anything you can find in the US with the antiquated, extortionist sickcare system there. (US citizens frequently struggle to wrap their heads around the high quality care and low costs or no costs for medical care in Portugal).

Fun fact: The term "medical bankruptcy" does not have a Portuguese translation because it does not exist in Portugal. That's a uniquely US thing.

Most private insurance policies also include dental coverage, although paying cash for dental work is also common (and reasonable).

Important note: You will have to purchase private health insurance as part of your visa application. You will need to maintain that coverage and be able to show proof for your visa renewals, although you can use the SNS during that time if you wish. Once you become a permanent resident, you no longer need to carry private insurance coverage.

The reasons most expats cite for maintaining private insurance even after becoming citizens are so they can get faster care (sometimes there are long waits at the free healthcare facilities) and choosing a doctor they like who speaks English (there are plenty in the socialized system who speak English, though). There are many policies available for reasonable prices.

Taxes

The tax system in Portugal includes federal income, local, capital gains, and inheritance taxes. The corporate tax structure also includes a value added tax (VAT) system.

Income taxes

The good news for expats: Tax treaties exist between Portugal and the countries where many expats used to call home (including the US, UK and Canada) so those people can avoid double taxation on some or all of their income.

The bad news: Tax treaties can be complex and confusing, often resulting in hefty fees paid to accountants every year to be sure you are properly filing everything.

Non-residents of Portugal are only taxed on the income they earn in Portugal. So if you live in the US and have a beach house in Portugal that you use for one month of the year and rent the other eleven months of the year, Portugal will only tax you on your rental income from the beach house (although the US may want a piece as well, depending on your situation). Any additional money you earn in the US would not be subject to taxation in Portugal.

Be careful here: Spending 183 days a year or more in Portugal can make you a tax resident by default, which could make your tax bill(s) very large and very messy.

To make it even more complicated, if you maintain a property in Portugal and spend less than 183 days there every year BUT it looks to the authorities like that is your primary home, you will be treated as a tax resident. It is at their discretion whether or not to classify you as a tax resident or not. So maybe don't get close to those 183 days unless you want to become a tax resident in Portugal, eh?

UPDATED 2022: Here are the income tax rates in Portugal (in euros):

Taxable income	Rate
0 - 7116	14.5%
7117 - 10,736	23%
10,737 - 15,216	26.5%
15,217 - 19,696	28.5%
19,697 - 25,076	35%
25,077 - 36,757	37%
36,758 - 48,033	43.5%
48,034 - 75,009	45%

75,010 +   48%

Non-Habitual Residency (NHR)

NHR is one of the most popular elements of moving to Portugal that is enjoyed by expats. The gist of it is most people can live in Portugal for ten years while only paying a flat income rate of 20%, and no tax on worldwide income.

You have to apply for this status (it's not automatic), and it can be denied if your application is incomplete or filed after the deadline.

UPDATED 2021: Foreign retirees now have to pay taxes on their foreign-sourced pension income (10%).

It is always a good idea to enlist the help of a tax professional who can help you with your taxes to be sure you are filing properly in Portugal, and anywhere else in the world where you may need to file (looking mostly at the US citizens here).

VAT (value added tax)

The VAT rate in Portugal is variable. The standard rate is 23%, the reduced rate is 6% and the intermediate rate is 13%. There is a slight variation to these rates on the Azores and Madeira Islands. Azores charges 18%, 10% and 5%, and Madeira charges 22%, 12% and 5%.

The VAT rates for most of Portugal are the following:

- Standard rate: 23% for goods and services
- Intermediate rate: 13% for some food products, restaurants, wine, bottled water, admission to cultural sites and events
- Reduced rate: 6% for other food products, newspapers, some prescription drugs, some medical supplies, hotels, legal services, social services, some medical and dental services, private passenger transportation and various other random products and services

IMI (Imposto Municipal sobre Imóveis)

IMI is a local tax that is only paid by property owners. The IMI tax rate varies on the general wealth of the area—wealthy areas pay more and poorer areas pay less. The tax revenue goes to municipal services such as maintaining roads, trash collection, etc.

The rates are 0.3% to 0.45% for homes in urban areas and 0.8% for properties in rural areas. If the property is owned by a corporation in a known tax haven such as the Cayman Islands, Gibraltar, Jersey, Isle of Man, etc., the IMI tax rate will be 7.5%.

For people who own homes worth more than €600,000, there is a higher IMI rate. You can think of it as a luxury tax or a wealth tax.

IMT (Imposto Municipal sobre a Transmissão Onerosa de Imóveis)

The IMT is the property transfer tax, which is paid as part of the property acquisition process. It applies to property purchases, and corporate share purchases if the corporation's main purpose is the ownership of property in Portugal.

There are two primary categories of property subject to IMT—property for use as a primary residence, and property for use as a non-permanent residence (like a second home).

The tax rates vary depending upon the value of the property at the time of purchase. The rates for primary residences range from 0-8% and the rates for non-permanent residences range from 1-8%.

There are some variations in the IMT rates for properties that are not being used as residences by the owners. Rural properties pay 5%, commercial buildings pay 6.5% and properties purchased by people in known tax havens pay 15%.

AIMI (Adicional ao Imposto Municipal sobre Imóveis a.k.a. "wealth tax")

The AIMI is different from the IMI and requires a separate payment. It applies to most properties valued over €600,000.

The rates are calculated in several tiers:

- Property valued from €600,000 to €1,000,000 = 0.7%
- Property valued from €1,000,000 to €2,000,000 = 1.0%
- Property valued more than €2,000,000 = 1.5%

Inheritance tax

As a general rule, there is no inheritance tax for immediate relatives in Portugal. There are some exceptions, of course.

For example, your will could say one thing, but your spouse and children may have rights to your estate in Portugal even if you have tried to exclude them in the will. This only applies if some of your estate is subject to Portuguese inheritance laws.

The inheritance tax laws in Portugal are determined by the home country of the deceased person. It can get a little tricky for people married to someone with a different nationality.

Should people outside your immediate family members inherit any of your assets in Portugal, they will be subject to a 10% stamp duty. This stamp duty only applies to assets in Portugal, though.

If any stamp duty or inheritance tax is due, it must be paid within three months of the death in order to avoid late penalties and interest.

It is always wise to enlist the help of qualified estate planning attorneys when preparing a will. It is extra important to have all your ducks in a row if you have assets in multiple countries or have immediate relatives with different nationalities than you.

Primary, Secondary & Higher Education

High-quality education can be found throughout Portugal. International schools are the top choices for most expats due to the enriching multicultural experiences provided for the students. The schools come in various sizes, price ranges and approaches to education. There are also public schools and private schools available that follow a traditional Portuguese curriculum.

The international schools are mostly located in and around Lisbon and Cascais, with a few outliers in Porto and the Algarve. They follow the International Baccalaureate standards that prepare students for admission in the top universities in the world.

Portuguese is taught in some form in all the schools. Some parents help their children prepare for the move by enrolling them in video Portuguese language tutoring before they arrive. English is the primary language in international schools.

Primary and secondary education

These are a few of the most popular schools in the expat community:

CAISL (Carlucci American International School of Lisbon) is a popular option with expats. The school serves grades K-12 and the language of instruction is English. There are just over 700 students and 92 full-time faculty members. Portuguese, French, Spanish and Chinese languages are all offered at the school.

TASIS Portugal is the newest school in the TASIS family of schools. TASIS Switzerland was the first American boarding school in Europe back in the 1950s. They plan to serve grades pre-K to grade 7 in their inaugural year of 2020-2021 with plans to add grade 8 in 2021.

St. Julian's is a British international school located in Carcavelos. They serve all ages from nursery to grade 12 and have a strong academic track record. They were founded in 1932 and boast a large and active alumni network all over the world.

Redbridge School in Lisbon is an international primary school with a focus on multilingual education. They have a very low teacher to student ratio and use a Montessori style approach to education.

Oeiras International School serves all age groups and follows the International Baccalaureate standards. They have a unique approach that includes students formally being involved in service projects, and a guided personal project during grade 11.

Waldorf school in the Algarve (Escola Livre do Algarve) is located in Lagos and was opened in 2008. They are currently focused on primary school education and they are hoping to offer education to the higher grades in the near future.

British School of Lisbon is part of The Schools Trust (TST), which is a UK-registered non-profit. They follow the English National Curriculum that is recognized for its academic rigor around the world.

International Preparatory School (IPS) has a multilingual staff and focuses on a well-rounded education involving issues of global importance. It is located close to Cascais and serves students from nursery age to age eleven.

Higher education

Portugal is home to a few dozen universities and polytechnic institutions. They offer a variety of programs including master's and doctoral programs. Admissions to the state-run universities are competitive and based largely on previous academic performance.

The university system dates back to the 13th century. There are currently thirteen public universities, one public university institute, a public open university and a few private universities.

The polytechnic system we developed in the 1980s. They were developed in response to the changing needs of the workforce. There are currently fifteen polytechnic institutes run by the state, and many more institutes that have various areas of vocational and technical focus.

Starting a business in Portugal

The mechanics for opening a business in Portugal are similar to what you find in most other countries. You'll need to obtain a tax identification number, register for VAT, get a bank account and register your company with the applicable levels of government. It's wise to get professional help from a lawyer and accountant for all of these steps.

The corporate tax rate in Portugal is 21% on the mainland, 20% in Madeira and 16.8% in Azores. Portugal only taxes corporate income that is generated from business activity in Portugal. Income generated from abroad could be considered non-taxable in Portugal (clarify this with your accountant if you have questions).

Business expenses and operating costs can be deducted from the total when figuring the taxable income, and you will be responsible for regular filings and tax installment payments. Again, you'll want to get help with this from an accountant.

Starting a brick and mortar business

A surfing camp. A tour company. A wine bar. A yoga retreat venue. A bed and breakfast. All of these are wonderful ideas that could fund your life in Portugal and give you something to do with your time.

The process for opening a business that requires a physical location in Portugal is similar to what you'll experience in most other countries. You'll have to navigate commercial zoning laws, local business registration, taxes, payroll, etc. Commercial leases have a high degree of complexity in Portugal as well.

There's certainly nothing wrong with opening a brick and mortar business, but it shouldn't be confused with an entity that will print money for you without your participation.

Which brings us to...

Starting an online business

Many people work remotely in Portugal. They either run their own online businesses or work for a company that gives them the flexibility to work from wherever they please.

The dream of starting an online business has never been easier to achieve. It doesn't need to be the next Amazon or Microsoft in order to fund a nice life. Here's how to get started in only a few hours.

Why start an online business? Freedom, flexibility and money are the three reasons online entrepreneurs cite the most. They want to harvest money from the internet, make their own hours and work from whatever location suits them best that day.

Some people leave their day jobs to start an online business and very quickly end up broke! This happens when they go a little too heavy on the freedom and flexibility without enough focus on the making money part.

It's easy to get lost down rabbit holes of things that feel like work, but don't actually make you any money. Tasks like endlessly optimizing website designs or logos or complex sales funnels are common ways to burn days or weeks.

Don't be one of the people who is "getting ready to get ready" forever. You don't have an online business until it's making money for you. Until then, it's just a hobby.

Once you've decided it's time to get started, it's just a matter of putting the pieces together. People have lived before you and there's no need to reinvent the wheel.

Step one: Figure out what you are going to sell

You have a choice here. You can either find a product someone else has made and sell it on your website, or you can create a product of your own to sell on your website.

Creating your own product takes some time and energy, but the benefits are significant. It also gives you a degree of control that you don't have when you're relying on someone else to create what you're selling.

For example, selling N95 face masks might seem like a great business these days. The people who had businesses selling these masks during the coronavirus pandemic ran into some challenges. The demand was through the roof! Great news, right?

Not quite.

There were some challenges filling orders from customers. The government was seizing any new shipments of N95 masks instead of letting them be shipped to their intended recipients.

To make it even more complicated, Facebook and Google banned all advertising for N95 masks (even from legitimate companies who had been advertising them for years). They had to do that because the scammers and price gougers showed up en masse when the coronavirus panic began. The problem was this policy ALSO harmed the legitimate sellers.

That's an extreme example, but you get the idea. You are always at risk if you are selling someone else's product. It's better to have your own product to sell, whether that's a physical product or a digital product.

Informational products are perfect items to sell on the internet. If your final product is an ebook or a course or an instructional video series, you can sell an infinite number of them after doing the work of creating it. Plus, it's easier to maintain a website than it is to manage physical inventory, production, shipping, returns, etc.

A common response here is, "But I don't have any special knowledge that anyone would pay for!"

You might be surprised.

I would argue that everybody has something of value they could teach others, no matter how obscure or unimportant or basic the knowledge might seem to you.

Some examples of informational products that sell well are cookbooks, Excel templates, personal finance guides and how-to courses for even the most basic subjects (think about how popular the For Dummies books have become...nothing is too basic). Somebody out there wants the knowledge you possess and it's your job to make it easy for them to find you on the internet.

The easiest informational products are the ones that don't take much or any technical skill to create. Which one of these do you think would be easiest for you? Pick one and start there.

Online courses: A combination of text, audio and video content is the preferred delivery method these days. There are some free Wordpress plugins (more on Wordpress later) that will do all the heavy lifting around the course structure and such. All you need to do is add the content. You can charge a flat fee per course

Ebooks: Like the one you are reading right now! You can sell ebooks on your own website as well and many people do so with great success. I like the Kindle store because I can lean on Amazon's massive distribution reach. Ebooks don't need to be as robust as full-length paperback books and they can focus on the most obscure topics imaginable.

Membership websites: This sort of business is a bit more involved because it requires some ongoing work in order for the value to be there for the members. The general idea is that you provide premium content of some sort that your users can access for a monthly membership fee. Many successful membership sites make some of their content available to everyone for free, and charge money for the premium content. These are good if you have some specific knowledge about a topic. Again, Wordpress has some free plugins that make the membership features easy to implement.

Online events or webinars: These businesses are great alternatives to in-person events and seminars. People are willing to pay for high-quality content. Live events are one approach, and you can also record webinars and events to sell over and over in the future.

Once you have decided on your first product to create, it's time for the next step.

Step two: Buy a domain name

There are a bunch of places that will sell you a domain name. A domain name is the .com, .net, .info, etc. that people will use to find you and your website. The domain name for our main website that helps people buy and sell real estate abroad is espatriati.com.

There are some important nuances to understand here. If at all possible, you want to find a domain with an extension that is a .com instead of a .net, .info, .news or any of the other dozens of options that have appeared over the past few years.

We originally went with .io for all of our domain names because we could keep it uniform across all of our web properties. Once the business had succeeded at a high enough level for a few years, we bit the bullet and purchased a .com. There's no right or wrong here, but I would suggest not trying to be too clever with some of the bizarre extensions that are out there.

Also, try to keep the name short, simple, easy to spell and easy to pronounce. Assume that every visitor to your site will have no more than an eighth-grade education.

I understand many of the "good" .com names are taken. You can get some creative ideas by using a thesaurus if needed. A simple solution for many people is to buy your firstnamelastname.com, assuming you have a unique enough name that it isn't taken yet.

The domain registrar I recommend is GoDaddy. WARNING: GoDaddy will try to upsell you all sorts of things you don't need, like hosting, email, privacy (privacy is a maybe for you), etc. Decline all of it. Just pick your domain name and skip ahead to the checkout page. Also, you only have to register the domain for one year at a time, even though their default at check out will be five years. They are tricky like that.

Step three: Get a quality hosting account

Website files need a place to live and the companies that provide this service are called web hosts.

Buy this today: WP Engine is the best hosting provider I have found for the purpose of running an online business. They are the right combination of quality, price and AMAZING customer service. I've bothered them with so many random questions and they always find a way to help. (Check our website for a discount link for WP Engine)

This is especially important if you are not super technical. They have tutorials and live chat help for anything you'll need to do with your website.

They also make it easy to handle things like unexpected surges in website traffic, DDOS attacks and making regular backups of your site in case something goes wrong. You can make changes in your website in "developer" mode, so the world won't see you experimenting with it. The customer support is top-notch as well (I like the Live Chat support function the best).

Once you have your hosting account, follow their instructions to connect your domain name from GoDaddy to your hosting account at WP Engine. They have tutorials and they make it easy for you.

Step four: Install WordPress and a WordPress theme

This is my favorite step because it doesn't cost any money!

Wordpress is the framework that powers about one third of the websites in the world. It's FREE and easy to install through WP Engine. In fact, the "WP" in WP Engine comes from Wordpress. They have all the support you'll need if you can't figure out how to do it yourself, but it's not hard. It should only take you a few minutes and a few clicks.

Once you've installed WordPress, you will want to install a theme. A theme is what makes your website pretty. There are a gazillion free themes out there and a bunch of paid options, too. It's best to pick a free one for now and worry about updating to a paid one after you're more comfortable with the specific needs of your online business.

You'll find the free themes inside the WordPress dashboard once you have installed WordPress on your domain. You'll be prompted to create a username and password when you install WordPress and they'll email you login credentials. To install a theme, go to your WordPress dashboard, click on Appearance, then Themes. You'll see a bunch of free theme options in there. (Again, WP Engine has in-depth walkthrough articles and a responsive support team if you get stuck.)

All the themes focus on different features and they can do different things. WordPress is a very flexible framework and there are solutions for everything you can imagine. Plus, most themes don't require any coding or programming experience to work with them.

Step five: Put a payment mechanism on your site

This step is also free. It will cost you nothing to create accounts with Paypal and Stripe. Go do that now.

Paypal is super simple and you probably already have an account with them. The easiest way to add payment options to your site for whatever you're selling is to add a Paypal button. You can follow the simple instructions inside your Paypal account for installing the button on your site.

Paypal will charge you a small percentage of your sales you make through the use of the Paypal button. You should also know that Paypal will take a few days to transfer money to your bank account when you're ready to collect your cash. It's mildly annoying, but you'll survive.

WARNING: Paypal has a nasty reputation if you make too many sales too fast. This is especially true if you have a new Paypal account and/or a new product you're selling with your Paypal button. Weird, right? I agree.

There are horror stories about people having their funds frozen by PayPal for weeks or months with no way to fix the problem (no phone number to call, emails and support messages are ignored). It's rare, but it happens. Paypal will probably work just fine forever for smaller projects, though. Consider yourself warned.

A better payment processing option once you have tested your product and it looks like people are ready to buy it is Stripe. Stripe takes a little more sophistication to implement on websites, but it's still on the easy end of the technical scale.

Like Paypal, they allow you to establish an account for free and they take a small percentage of your sales that are processed through them. Stripe links to your bank account and automatically deposits your earnings on a regular basis. They have a great dashboard that allows you to track everything as well.

Stripe is growing by leaps and bounds. They continue to make improvements in functionality and ease of use. They also have a robust FAQ and tutorial section to help you get started with the more technical bits.

There are also merchant accounts available through most traditional banks. Payment processing through merchant accounts with a traditional bank should be avoided at all costs. They are clunky, horrendously expensive and they use outdated technology.

Step six: Find customers

"If you build it, they will come."

Hahaha. Nope.

You'll have to find a way to get customers to your site so they have a chance to buy your product. It's great when customers find your product through channels that don't cost you any money, like word-of-mouth, social media posts or search engine results. In the beginning, it's unlikely that enough customers will find you through the free channels, so you'll have to spend some money.

Google and Facebook are the big dogs when it comes to finding customers online through advertising. They both have advertising products that allow you to target people based on certain parameters. There are plenty of tutorials that will help you learn their systems.

I suggest setting a low budget and capping the daily amount of money you can spend on ads when you first start. If you don't put a cap on it, Google and Facebook will definitely take all of your money. You can learn and see what works with a small budget, then increase your budget later once you know the math and know what works.

Step seven: Repeat as needed

There's power in being focused. Pushing on only one product is the best approach until your product is reliably selling at a rate that is acceptable to you.

One of the benefits of informational products is that you should be able to automate most or all of the selling once you get the hang of it. Once that happens, you'll have some time on your hands to create another product.

Creating a natural extension or "sequel" of your first product is usually a good way to do it. You already have customers, an email list and you know how the ads perform in your category. There's no need to start over with something unfamiliar when you have so much leverage from your first product. For example, we have a few other "Move to ___" guides in the works for some other popular countries right now. And they have the added bonus of complementing our primary business!

One of my favorite success stories from this approach is Robert Kiyosaki with his Rich Dad series of books, courses and games. He built a brand around personal finance and created multiple products around the same theme. Regardless of what you think about the guy as a person, he was a master at building a large brand with informational products.

That's it! You should be good to go.

Appendix 1: Preparation Checklist

Before you make the move to Portugal, you'll want to make sure you have all your ducks in a row. Getting your visa and finding a place to live are probably the biggest tasks you'll need to manage, but any international move has the potential to create hassles and headaches.

You may wish to create your own checklist or spreadsheet for tracking and these items should give you a good start.

- Is your passport up to date, with at least six months left before it expires?
- Have you made a copy of your passport and visa documentation to carry with you?
- Have you emailed yourself a copy of your passport and visa documentation?
- Have you contacted your bank and credit card companies to let them know you'll be out of the country?
- Do you have proof of travel insurance? (Travel insurance coverage through credit cards doesn't count)
- Do you have enough euros to get you to your initial destination, or currency that can be exchanged for euros if there are no working ATMs at the airport?
- Have you downloaded all the appropriate travel apps?

- Have you downloaded an offline map on your phone with directions to your initial destination?
- Have you recently confirmed your hotel or short-term stay reservations?
- Have you recently confirmed any rental car or private driver reservations?
- Do you have a battery pack for charging your phone? Is it fully charged?
- Do you have an international phone plan, or a phone where you can add a local SIM card when you arrive?
- If traveling with pets, do you have the pet passport and immunization documentation?
- Do you have all of your children with you? (I loved *Home Alone* when I was a kid)

Appendix 2: Useful smartphone apps

One of the greatest parts about living in Portugal is the easy access to so many wonderful destinations in other European and African countries. There's plenty to do and see in Portugal, although a quick trip to Spain or Morocco may always be tempting.

In our always-connected world, you will want to have a fairly new smartphone that can run all the latest apps. Here are a few apps that will make your life easier when you're traveling in or around Western Europe.

Waze is a wonderful app (owned by Google now). Keep in mind it requires a cell phone signal to work if you haven't downloaded the appropriate map before you leave an area with cell phone service.

Hopper is a flight booking app. It has a lovely interface that lets you pick two destinations and see the flight options months into the future in a calendar format. Each calendar date has a price on it and is coded with red (expensive for that route), yellow (average cost for that route) or green (cheap for that route). They allow you to set alerts for yourself if you want to watch a certain price and date that looks a little high and they will provide recommendations on whether you should book now or wait.

Google Translate is a free app that works like magic. You can easily type a word to translate into it and decide what language you'd like. Voila! That part is great, but the real magic is in the live camera translation function. Imagine being in a restaurant and they only have menus in Italian, but you don't speak Italian. No problem! Fire up your Google Translate app and push the camera icon. The app will TRANSLATE THE MENU IN ENGLISH IN REAL TIME. You really have to see it to believe it. They keep adding more support such as static photo translation and voice translation support.

Speak & Translate has saved me a few times over the years. Google has added some similar functionality as well. The way this works is you speak whatever you want to say in your normal English voice and in a few seconds, it will recite it back in Spanish (or whatever other language you choose). This is very handy when you're trying to communicate something in another language that requires some explanation. It costs a few euros to buy this app, but it's well worth it.

Duolingo is a great language learning app. It will help you get a head start on your Portuguese, and dozens of other languages. They have both free and paid versions. Start with the free version and see how far you get before you upgrade.

Ridesharing apps are a must-have these days. The big players in Portugal are Uber, Taxify and Cabify. Uber is one of the biggest and most popular in the world. One of the most common ways people get ripped-off when traveling is by taxi drivers (which is why Uber got started in the first place). Taxi drivers know they have suckers in the car who don't know the customary pricing or most direct routes to their destinations. Uber may or may not be legal in Portugal by the time you read this because taxi companies work very hard to keep Uber out of town. Uber was once banned in Portugal and is legal at the time of this writing (June 2020).

Uber Eats, Glovo, Takeaway.com, EatTasty. Order delivery food from your favorite restaurants through the apps (or mobile websites). Some of these services are only available in the bigger cities.

TripAdvisor is a good forum for all things travel, including restaurants, activities and local tips. You can also ask questions on the forum if you can't find an answer there.

Yelp is great for reading reviews from customers of shops, restaurants, bars and more! It isn't available in every country, though. Pro tip: You will also have to learn to read between the lines when reading restaurant reviews written by Americans who were on vacation. They have a tendency to criticize the level of service even if everything else was perfect and dock the restaurants a few stars. (They are used to servers working hard for tips and prompt service...not laid-back service).

HotelTonight: Book same-day hotels at steep discounts. Hotels put their excess inventory on the HotelTonight app. Bonus! If you use the code JSTERLING3 when you sign up, you get $25 off your first booking.

Here are a few more to consider, without the colorful descriptions:

Airbnb & VRBO: Great for short-term housing needs, and also their new "Experiences" section. **UPDATED 2022: While Airbnb and VRBO still work well for some people, they are not the utopia they used to be.**

In many parts of Portugal, the price for an Airbnb or VRBO is the same or more than what you would pay at a 4 or 5 star hotel, and you may find that you get an inferior experience. The mad rush to turn every available property into a short-term rental has created some junk in the short-term rental market. Tread lightly, and never book anything on Airbnb or VRBO unless it has dozens of positive reviews. There are lots of scams these days as well.

TripIt: Consolidates all of your travel itineraries in one place

WifiMapper: Find the closest wifi to you

Parting notes

Thank you for purchasing our guide! We hope it was helpful and informative. We will update it from time to time and the updates will appear automatically in your Kindle or Kindle app.

If you are happy with this guide, will you please take a minute to leave us a review on Amazon? The reviews are helpful and let other expats know the guide is legitimate. One or two sentences will do it. Thank you!

If you have questions we haven't answered or something that needs clarification, please email portugal@espatriati.com and we will find the answer for you, or help you find the person who has the answer. Many of the updates we add from time to time come from our readers' email questions, so please don't be shy!

Also, we have created a checklist for moving to Portugal. It includes everything you need to do regarding the application, appointments, etc. We would be happy to share that with you. Send us a quick note at portugal@espatriati.com and we'll send it over.

Made in United States
Cleveland, OH
03 December 2024